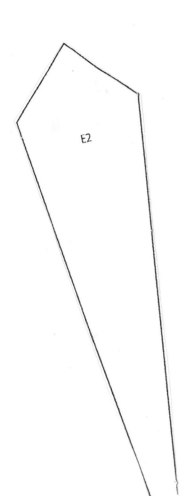

E2

DISTINCTIVE DRESDENS

Distinctive Dresdens

26 Intriguing Blocks, 6 Projects

KATJA MAREK

Distinctive Dresdens: 26 Intriguing Blocks, 6 Projects
© 2017 by Katja Marek

Martingale®
19021 120th Ave. NE, Ste. 102
Bothell, WA 98011-9511 USA
ShopMartingale.com

Printed in China
22 21 20 19 18 17   8 7 6 5 4 3 2 1

Library of Congress Cataloging-in-Publication Data is available upon request.

ISBN: 978-1-60468-852-8

MISSION STATEMENT

We empower makers who use fabric and yarn to make life more enjoyable.

CREDITS

PUBLISHER AND CHIEF VISIONARY OFFICER
Jennifer Erbe Keltner

CONTENT DIRECTOR
Karen Costello Soltys

MANAGING EDITOR
Tina Cook

ACQUISITIONS EDITOR
Karen M. Burns

TECHNICAL EDITOR
Angela Ingle

COPY EDITOR
Melissa Bryan

DESIGN MANAGER
Adrienne Smitke

PRODUCTION MANAGER
Regina Girard

COVER AND INTERIOR DESIGNER
Kathy Kotomaimoce

PHOTOGRAPHER
Brent Kane

ILLUSTRATOR
Sandy Huffaker
Linda Schmitz

SPECIAL THANKS

Thanks to Cassie Barden and Jon LeCroy of Seattle, Washington, for allowing the photography for this book to take place in their home.

DEDICATION

To my friend Linda King, who suggested what seems like so long ago now, "Why don't you write a book?"

And to my mom, Sonja Marek; without her, I'd accomplish much less in quilting and in life. She once again pitched in to help appliqué many of the Distinctive Dresden blocks in this book.

Contents

Introduction   6

Tools and Equipment   8

Techniques for Distinctive Dresdens   11

THE BLOCKS   25

THE PROJECTS   53

     Good Morning Place Mats   55

     Paper Lanterns Wall Quilt   59

     Merry Christmas Tree Skirt   63

     Clamoring for More Quilt   67

     Over the Edge Table Runner   73

     Class-Act Cushions   77

Quiltmaking Basics   81

Patterns   86

Resources   94

Acknowledgments   95

About the Author   96

Introduction

Throughout my life, whether poring over small quilt-block designs or large-scale house plans, I have never hesitated about changing what I found to make it more functional and pleasing to my eye—in other words, making it distinctive or notable. I took this approach when exploring the possibilities inside the hexagon for *The New Hexagon: 52 Blocks to English Paper Piece* and *The New Hexagon Perpetual Calendar* (Martingale, 2014 and 2016, respectively). For the blocks in those publications, I wanted to use the hexagon in a different manner than I had seen and used it previously. Now the story continues with Dresden Plates.

During a meeting of a quilt group in my shop, we decided to have a challenge. We called it "traditional made modern." I immediately had ideas flowing through my head about all the ways this theme could be put into action with the Dresden Plate block, but I kept getting stuck on the idea of *changing* the block. I asked myself why the Dresden Plate always had to have equal-sized petals, when there are so many more possibilities.

Distinctive: having a special quality, style, attractiveness, etc.; notable.

—DICTIONARY.COM

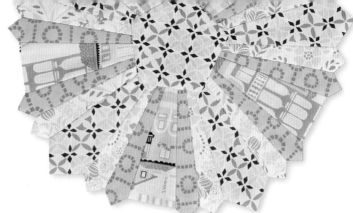

The Dresden Plate quilt block takes its name from the German town of Dresden, which popularized beautiful, elaborate porcelain plates painted with floral designs, fruits, and foliage. Blocks inspired by these ornate plates were among the most popular quilt blocks during the 1920s and '30s. Traditionally they consisted of twenty 18° petals radiating from the middle, with a circle appliquéd to the center. The design was also known by other names such as Grandmother's Sunbursts, Sunflower, Aster, Dahlia, and Friendship Rings. Although the name Dresden Plate didn't come into use until the 1920s, similar blocks existed well before this time. The Grandmother's Fan block created in the 1800s was simply one-quarter of a plate block in which the petals often had straight ends, unlike the pointed or rounded blades of the Dresden Plate.

In 2015, I visited Dresden and had the opportunity to visit the nearby Meissen porcelain factory and the Museum of Meissen Art, with displays covering more than 300 years of porcelain history. I saw firsthand the porcelain this town is so famous for and was struck by its beauty and diversity. Again I wondered why the blocks named for this spectacular china were not also as diverse.

In this book, I have tried to provide an answer to my own question. I wanted to create very distinctive blocks containing wedges with multiple and varying angles, sometimes with points inserted between the wedges for interest. To achieve this, I developed a system using the precise paper shapes that are so effective for English paper piecing, combined with the option of machine piecing to easily insert pointed fabric pieces between the wedges. By bringing together my beloved English paper piecing, precise paper templates, and machine piecing for a new approach, I have added exciting new chapters to the story.

So experience the diverse, become distinctive, and dare to be different with *Distinctive Dresdens.*

Katja

© MEISSEN®

An array of supplies to have on hand for making Distinctive Dresden blocks

Tools and Equipment

Tools and equipment are an important part of the quilting process, whether you are piecing by hand or by machine. The following products are readily available, and I've used them successfully to make all the projects in this book (refer to "Resources" on page 94 for the product websites).

Paper

I print my patterns onto cover stock paper. I find it's the ideal weight for English paper piecing, and it's also perfect for machine piecing when I add inserts because it allows me to easily feel and align the edges of the paper templates. It's flexible enough to bend at intersecting seams in traditional English paper piecing, and sturdy enough to give a nice sharp edge for closed glue basting (page 15). As an alternative, precut papers for English paper piecing are available from the company Paper Pieces (see "Die-Cut Paper Pieces" on page 13).

Marking Tools

I use a fine-line water-soluble marking pen from Collins for marking all except the darkest fabrics, in which case I use a Clover white marking pen; both of these can be removed with water. For simple straight lines, I use a Hera marker (also from Clover), a gadget that looks like a small spatula and allows you to place pressure when marking on fabric. These are the tools I used for marking all the projects in this book.

Basting Glue

I've often said that glue revolutionized my life. I prefer glue over thread basting because it saves time and streamlines the process. I use the Fons & Porter water-soluble fabric glue stick. This refillable stick has a surface area only slightly more than ¼" in diameter, much smaller than a traditional glue marker, which makes it perfect for glue basting your seam allowances. The adhesive goes on blue and dries clear, so you can see where it has been applied and know that you have sufficient coverage. Another key factor is that this product is designed for use on fabric, ensuring that you will be able to remove the papers when needed. (Not all glue sticks work this way!)

Add-Three-Eighths Ruler

Using the Add-Three-Eighths ruler from CM Designs is the easiest way to achieve consistently accurate seam allowances while cutting out your fabrics. The ruler's ⅜" lip is easy to line up at the edge of the paper template to get precise results every time.

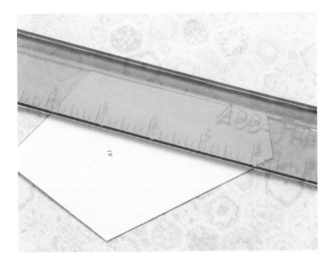

Needles

I use Clover Black Gold appliqué needles in size 10 for hand sewing. These were given to me as a sample to try, and I find they stand up to my usual tendency to bend or snap needles. They're very sharp and glide through the fabric easily.

Thread

There is great division over what type of thread to use for both hand and machine sewing. Since writing *The New Hexagon,* I have been asked to test various threads and have found the following to be my favorites: Mettler Silk Finish 50-weight 100% cotton, Aurifil 50-weight 100% cotton (available in a fabulous selection of colors), Superior MasterPiece 50-weight 100% cotton (which comes in a handy storage ring of prewound bobbins in 35 colors), and Wonderfil's InvisaFil 100-weight 2-ply cottonized polyester (which is so thin, yet strong, that it sinks in and becomes virtually invisible). My favorite thread color for machine piecing is medium gray, but for whipstitching while English paper piecing, I switch to a coordinating color. When appliquéing my Dresden blocks to a background fabric, I match the thread color to the fabric of the block.

Needle Threader

Having a needle threader handy can make many a sewing job easier. I've come to that point in my life where I can't seem to do without one. Although I use the Clover desk needle threader, you may discover that the Sewline handheld threader, or any traditional simple needle threader, will work for you.

Tailor's Awl

I find that a straight tailor's awl is the most effective tool for removing the glue-basted papers. It is also handy for pushing out the points of the covered-back wedges in the Over the Edge Table Runner (page 73).

Best Press

Before I remove the paper templates from pieces that will be appliquéd to a background, I use a pressing agent such as Mary Ellen's Best Press. This product is a starch and sizing alternative that gives a nice sharp edge to my work and allows it to maintain its shape even when the papers are no longer in place.

Appliqué Pins

Appliqué pins are short pins (usually about ¾" long) used to hold appliqué shapes in position on a background or on other fabric pieces. The advantage of these little pins over regular pins is that there is less pin for the thread to tangle around. Thread often gets caught on the head or point of long pins, which can be very frustrating. I prefer pins with a rounded head, such as Clover appliqué pins, which reduce the chance of tangling during appliqué.

On-the-Go Box

Although some of my work in these Dresden blocks is done by machine, much of it is done by hand, so I like to have a box ready with all my supplies for English paper piecing and appliqué. You can use a plastic container with a lid that fits firmly, or something fancier if you choose. A 9" × 12" box that's 2" or 3" high will fit everything you need.

Your on-the-go box should contain all the essentials, including small paper scissors, small sharp fabric scissors, needles, needle threader, thread, water-soluble marking pen, glue stick and refill, paper for making patterns, and a small selection of fabrics for piecing.

Basting Spray

I don't have the time or inclination to spend hours thread or pin basting quilt layers prior to quilting, but I have discovered that using 505 Temporary Fabric Adhesive from Odif USA is a great solution. I save time and don't have to deal with the unsightly holes that safety pins have occasionally left in my quilts, especially when I have been working with tightly woven fabrics like batiks.

SORTING AND STORING TEMPLATES

Whether you choose to make your own paper templates or purchase die-cut templates from Paper Pieces, the templates need to be sorted and stored. I've found simple zipper-seal sandwich bags are perfect for this task. I write the template name on a sticky note, which I place inside the bag so that it doesn't accidentally peel off.

This also works very well for groups of acrylic or plastic templates, in which case I keep similar groups in the same bag and list every template in the bag on the label (A1, A2, A3, and so on).

Before storing, verify the template sizes by placing them over the patterns on pages 83–93. Be sure to check both the side length and the angle, as these differ from block to block.

Techniques for Distinctive Dresdens

While designing my Dresden blocks, I knew I wanted them to have a look that is special and distinctive. I *love* the accuracy and precision of the die-cut paper shapes used for English paper piecing, but I felt that a new approach, using new techniques, was required to make everything come together as I envisioned. As a result, I've created two techniques for which I've coined the terms "open glue basting" and "closed glue basting." These are the two ways I prepare the pieces for doing English paper piecing by hand (closed) and by machine (open). I use open glue basting when I need to insert fabrics between two wedges in the Dresden ring. That may sound as clear as mud at the moment, but I'll show you how to accomplish all these techniques and more in this section. Then you'll be ready to create your own Distinctive Dresdens!

Preparing Paper Templates

1. Choose the block or blocks needed for your project from "The Blocks" on pages 25–51, and note the templates needed for each one. Each project indicates the specific blocks I used for the featured sample, but general guidelines are also provided about what type or types of blocks are needed, allowing you the freedom to select your own designs.

2. Photocopy the required quantities of the wedge and center patterns for each block (pages 86–93) onto cover stock. If one or more of your blocks includes insert pieces, make one photocopy of pattern I (page 91).

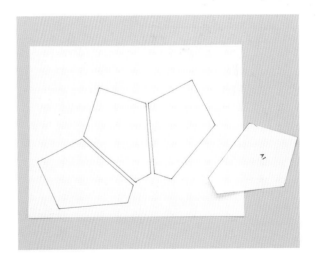

Distinctive Dresden Block Anatomy

Wedge. A kite-shaped fabric piece. Wedges vary in width from wide to narrow.

Facet. A group of wedges that repeats within a block. The blocks in this book have 2, 3, 4, 5, or 6 facets (see pages 25–51).

Insert. A folded fabric piece that's machine stitched between two facets and then pressed flat to create a dimensional triangle (see the instructions starting on page 18 and the photo below). Some blocks have inserts; others do not.

Center. A fabric shape (or shapes) appliquéd atop the center of the joined facets, covering the raw ends of the wedges (and inserts, if any).

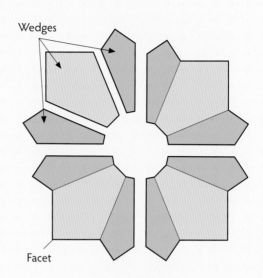

Wedges

Facet

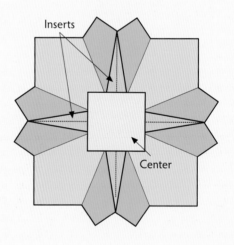

Inserts

Center

Wedge

Insert

3. To make templates, cut along the outline of each photocopied pattern, trimming away and discarding the excess paper. Cutting through the center of the printed lines (instead of cutting outside the lines or cutting off the lines completely) will achieve the most accurate blocks.

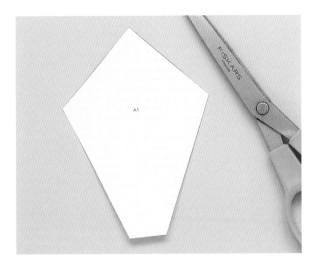

DIE-CUT PAPER PIECES

The instructions in this section describe how to make your own paper templates, and then how to use them. If you'd prefer to skip steps 2 and 3, you can instead purchase die-cut paper pieces to make each of the blocks in this book. Look for "Distinctive Dresdens: Complete Block Piecing Pack" at your local quilt shop or online at paperpieces.com.

The die-cut templates are not labeled, so before using them be sure to label each piece with its template letter and number, referring to the patterns on pages 86–93. When you sort and select the die-cut pieces for each block, verify that each piece matches its corresponding pattern.

---

4. Lay out all the paper templates for each block as it will be pieced, placing the center template(s) and the I insert template (if applicable) to the side.

Basting the Pieces

Before pieces are stitched into a Dresden block, the long side edges of each wedge piece (patterns A1–G2) must be glue basted with either the open or closed technique. The point of all wedge pieces and each center appliqué piece (patterns J–Q) must be closed glue basted.

In *open glue basting,* a template is adhered to the fabric, but the seam allowance is left unturned, or open. This technique is used for wedge seams that will be stitched by machine to accommodate a fabric insert. In addition, if you wish to join any other wedges by machine (instead of whipstitching them together by hand), you'll need to open glue baste the long edges of each wedge to be machine pieced.

In *closed glue basting,* a template is adhered to the fabric, and then the seam allowance is turned under and adhered to the back of the paper template. This technique is used for seams that will be whipstitched by hand (as for traditional English paper piecing) or edges that will be appliquéd to a background.

Open Glue Basting

Pointed inserts between the wedges of the Dresden blocks add interest, but appliquéing their sharp points can be difficult. Sewing those seams by machine instead makes this process a breeze. Seams that have a pointed insert sewn between the wedges (or any seam that you wish to machine piece) need to be open glue basted, which is exactly what it sounds like: the paper template is glued to the fabric with temporary fabric glue, but the seam allowances are left open, not folded around the edge of the paper.

1. Place a paper template facedown. Using a glue stick, apply glue along the perimeter of the template with a slightly heavier hand than you might normally use for glue basting. Place several lines of glue in the center of the template as well.

2. Position the template, glue side down, onto the wrong side of your chosen fabric. Hold the template in place momentarily with your fingertips until it is adhered.

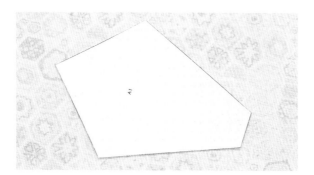

3. Cut out the fabric shape, adding ⅜" seam allowance all around the paper template. (I use the Add-Three-Eighths ruler for this step; see page 9. If you don't have an Add-Three-Eighths ruler, use a regular rotary-cutting ruler that has ⅛" markings.)

4. For any edge that will be machine pieced, leave the seam allowance flat, or open. For edges that will be whipstitched to other pieces by hand or appliquéd to a background, refer to the following instructions for closed glue basting.

CRUCIAL: A CONSISTENT ⅜" SEAM ALLOWANCE

For English paper piecing, experience has taught me that a ⅜" seam allowance is preferable to a ¼" one. Part of the seam allowance is taken up in the fold around the edge of the paper, and after investing time and money on your projects you don't want to end up short of seam allowance, leaving your seams vulnerable to fraying.

The blocks in this book require a combination of machine piecing, English paper piecing, and appliqué. Since all the machine sewing is done along the edge of the paper templates (instead of measuring from the edge of the fabric with the presser foot), a consistent seam allowance of ⅜" is of prime importance. If the raw fabric edges are aligned, you'll automatically know that the paper template edges are also aligned.

Closed Glue Basting

Any fabric edge that will be whipstitched with traditional English paper piecing or appliquéd to a background—including the points of all the wedges—needs to be closed glue basted.

1. Following steps 1–3 of "Open Glue Basting" on page 14, adhere a template to your chosen fabric and cut out the fabric shape, adding a ⅜" seam allowance. For this method, it's not necessary to apply glue to the perimeter of the template; just lightly apply a few lines of glue near the center.

2. Apply a line of glue on the step 1 template *near* an edge that will be whipstitched or appliquéd. Stay away from the actual paper edge, since trying to whipstitch through the glue can be difficult. For more accurate basting, add a dab of glue to the fabric along the side of the paper if the adjacent seam allowance will also be closed glue basted.

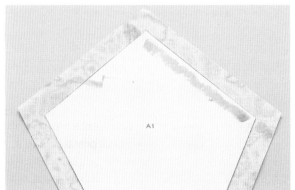

SOFT GLUE

In warm weather the glue stick can become a little soft, making it difficult to apply the correct amount. Simply pop the stick into the refrigerator for a few minutes to let the glue harden a bit, and then proceed as usual.

3. Finger-press the fabric edge onto the glue line and hold momentarily until secure.

4. Repeat steps 2 and 3 to glue baste each fabric edge around the template that will be whipstitched or appliquéd. (The open center of the Dresden ring will have another piece of fabric appliquéd over it, so the short bottom edge of each wedge piece doesn't need to be glued.)

Joining Wedges with English Paper Piecing

1. Lay out all the basted wedges for your selected block in sections, or *facets*. The facets represent how the wedges will be pieced together into a block, as shown in the first of the two diagrams for each block (pages 25–51). In this example, we have three facets, each with four wedges.

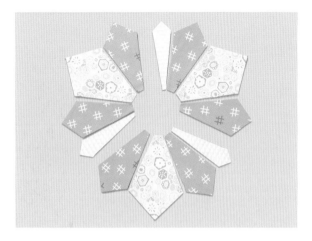

2. Thread your needle with a single strand of thread and tie a knot in the end.

3. Select two adjoining closed-glue-basted wedges from the same facet. On the paper side of one wedge, insert the needle under the seam allowance. Bring the needle out at one corner and hide the knot under the fabric.

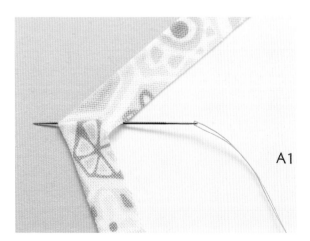

A1

4. Place the adjoining closed-glue-basted wedge atop the first wedge with right sides together. Align the edges to be joined and match the corners. Insert the needle through the point of the new piece from the wrong side of the piece.

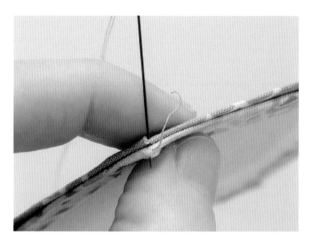

5. Whipstitch along the fold, making sure the needle enters the fabric perpendicular to the fabric edge. The thread will angle across the fold. This way very little thread will show on the finished side of your block. Take care to catch only one or two threads of fabric along the fold, using small stitches (about 12 stitches per inch). Do not stitch through the paper.

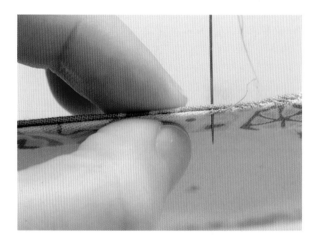

6. Secure the end of the stitching line with several locking backstitches as follows. At the end of your seam, place the needle through the fabric as though to take a stitch backward about ⅛" from the last stitch. From where the thread exits the fabric, run it behind the back (eye end) of the needle, then bring it up, over, and across the needle, and finally loop it around the tip of the needle. Pull the thread snugly to the needle before pulling the thread through to complete the stitch.

8. If the block has insert pieces, refer to "Adding Inserts" on page 18. If no inserts are needed, sew together all the facets with whipstitches to make a Dresden ring, and then proceed to "Completing the Blocks" on page 23.

DEALING WITH LOOSENED GLUE

Sometimes as we manipulate and work with glue-basted pieces, portions of the paper templates may separate from the fabric. If this happens, simply apply a little extra glue to the template to hold it in place until it is time to remove the papers.

7. Whipstitch the remaining closed-glue-basted wedges in the same manner to assemble each facet of the block.

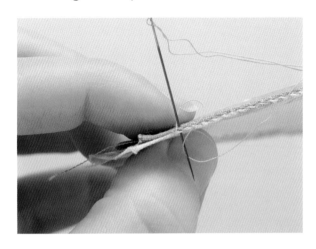

Adding Inserts

One of the distinctive aspects of the Dresdens in this book comes from the insert wedges. They let you add more colors, shapes, and texture to increase the "wow" factor of a basic Dresden Plate block. It's easier to sew in the inserts if all the wedges between the inserts are joined into facets first. This way the insert doesn't have to be pushed out of the way, possibly getting caught accidentally in seams when subsequent wedges are joined.

1. Any seam that has a pointed insert sewn between the facets or that will be pieced by machine should be open glue basted (page 14).

2. Using pattern I (page 91), cut the number of insert pieces needed for your selected block.

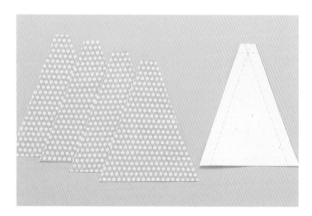

3. Fold down the tip of each insert piece ⅜" to the wrong side of the fabric and press.

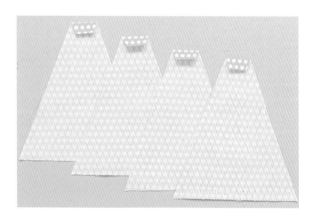

4. Fold each insert piece in half, *wrong* sides together and long raw edges aligned. Lightly finger-press the crease.

5. Select two assembled facets with open-glue-basted outer edges. Use your fingernail or a Hera marker (page 8) to score an indentation into the fabric right next to the paper template. This makes it easier to line up the pieces exactly where the seam allowances should come together.

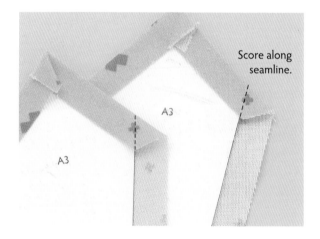

Score along seamline.

A3

A3

6. Place a prepared insert from step 4 between the scored pieces from step 5, lining up the raw edges, the score marks, and the edges of the paper templates.

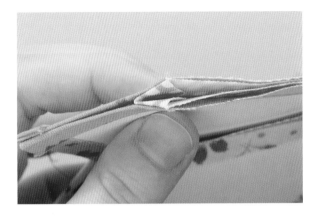

7. Machine stitch through all layers close to the edge of the paper templates, sewing from the top (pointed end) to the bottom (narrow end) of the wedges.

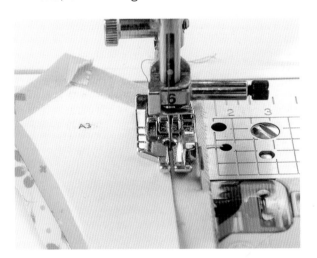

THREAD TAILS

At the top of the seam between the Dresden wedges, leave a tail of thread about 1" long. It is much easier to push a 1" thread tail under the edge of the block during appliqué than a short ⅛" tail. A wooden toothpick is a handy tool for tucking in these stray threads.

8. Open the joined facets. On the wrong side, open up and finger-press the seam allowance.

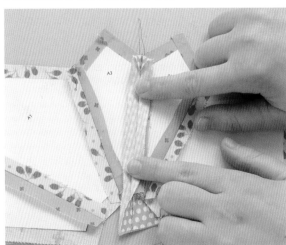

9. On the right side, line up the insert's finger-pressed crease with the underlying seam to create the pointed insert. Press.

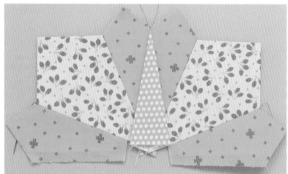

10. Repeat steps 5–9 to machine stitch the remaining inserts between the facets to make a Dresden ring. Trim the inserts even with the underlying wedges to reduce bulk. Proceed to "Completing the Blocks" on page 23.

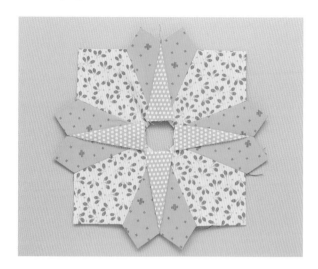

ASYMMETRICAL INSERTS

For blocks 16 and 25 (pages 41 and 50), the insert isn't centered and pressed flat, but instead is pressed to one side to create a pinwheel effect. This is indicated on the appropriate block diagrams with the label "I (asymmetrical)."

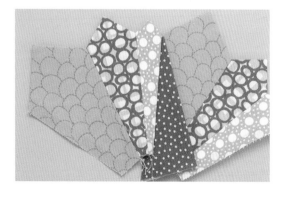

MACHINE PIECING WITHOUT PINNING

I've found that the more you bend the open-glue-basted shapes, the more likely the papers are to release from the fabric before you're ready to remove them. Pinning exacerbates this problem. As a solution, making a score mark on the fabric beside the paper template (step 5, page 18) offers an effective way to line up the edges of the paper templates. Also, if every seam is pieced and then immediately pressed open between the wedges, the paper templates tend not to release from the fabric before I am ready to remove them.

Making Covered-Back Wedges

The three blocks in the Over the Edge Table Runner on page 73 extend beyond the finished edge of the project, so the back of each extending wedge must be finished, or covered. Follow the steps below to make these wedges, and then refer to "Basting the Pieces" (page 13) to prepare them for stitching.

1. Photocopy and cut out the H precutting pattern (page 91) to make a paper template. Select any 4-faceted block from "The Blocks" on pages 25–51. For each of the block's wedges that will extend beyond the edges of the project, cut a piece of fabric using the H template.

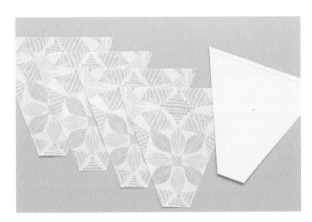

2. Fold a fabric H piece in half, right sides together and raw edges aligned. Lightly finger-press the crease.

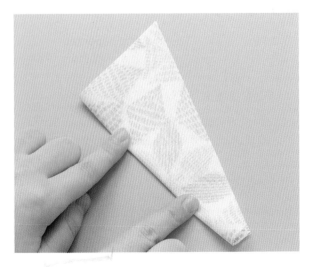

3. Machine sew the top edge, using a standard ¼" seam allowance.

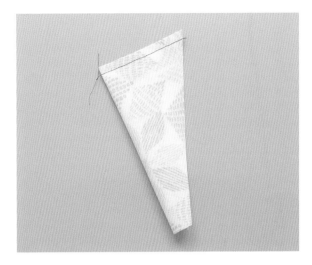

4. Unfold the piece, creating a point at the top edge. Open the seam allowance and finger-press.

5. Turn the point right side out and line up the seam with the finger-pressed crease. Use an awl, if necessary, to push out the point.

6. Glue the required wedge template for your selected block inside the point, referring to steps 1 and 2 of "Open Glue Basting" (page 14).

7. Trim any excess seam allowances to ⅜" to make a covered-back wedge. The H precutting template will accommodate the largest wedge pattern (A1) and will require trimming with all other wedges.

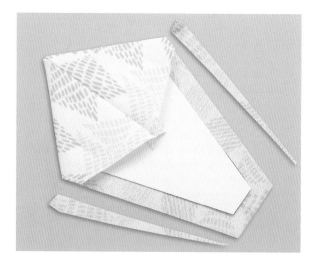

8. Repeat steps 2–7 to make the remaining covered-back wedges for the block.

Completing the Blocks

1. After all the wedges and any insert pieces are sewn together into a Dresden ring, it is time to remove the paper templates. Place the ring wrong side up on an ironing board and spray lightly with Best Press (page 9). Press until dry, making sure any corners and tails are folded over and pressed so they don't extend beyond the Dresden ring edge.

2. Turn the Dresden ring right side up, spray lightly with Best Press, and press again until dry.

3. Turn wrong side up and use an awl to loosen the pieces from their templates by sliding the tip under the fabric edges, between the fabric and the paper. Carefully remove the template papers.

4. Prepare the block-center appliqué with closed glue basting (page 15) and then press it with Best Press for a crisp, sharp edge. Remove the paper template as in step 3 below left.

5. Center the appliqué shape (or shapes) on the Dresden ring, referring to the appropriate block diagram for orientation. Pin in place with appliqué pins.

6. Referring to "Appliqué" on page 81 as needed, appliqué the piece in place to complete a Dresden Plate block.

Block 4

2-FACETED BLOCK

TEMPLATES NEEDED

Wedges:

4 of A1

4 of A2

4 of A5

Inserts: None

Center: 1 each of P and Q

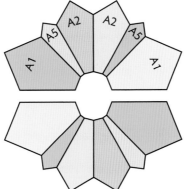

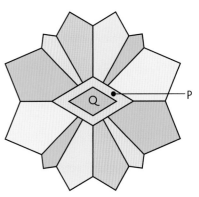

Block 5

2-FACETED BLOCK

TEMPLATES NEEDED

Wedges:

2 of A1

10 of A3

4 of A6

Inserts: None

Center: 1 of P

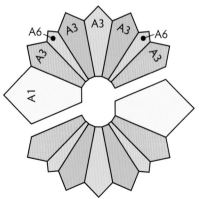

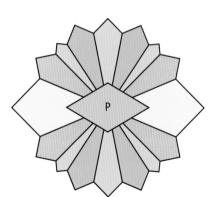

Block 12

TEMPLATES NEEDED

Wedges:
4 of B1
12 of B2
Inserts: None
Center: 1 of L

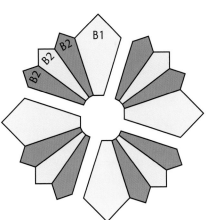

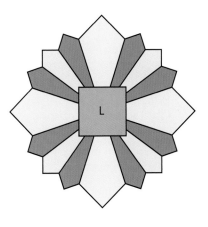

Block 13

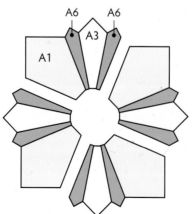

TEMPLATES NEEDED

Wedges:

4 of A1

4 of A3

8 of A6

Inserts: None

Center: 1 of L

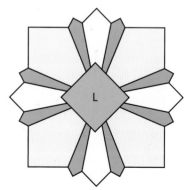

Block 14

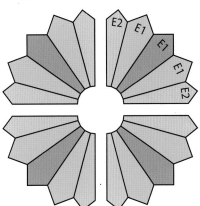

TEMPLATES NEEDED

Wedges:

12 of E1

8 of E2

Inserts: 4 of I

Center: 1 of L

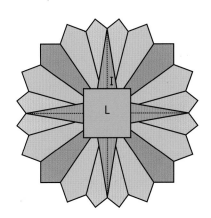

Block 15

TEMPLATES NEEDED

Wedges:

8 of D1

12 of D2

Inserts: 4 of I

Center: 1 of L

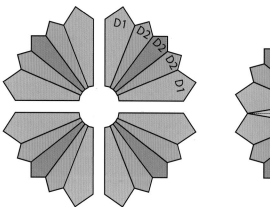

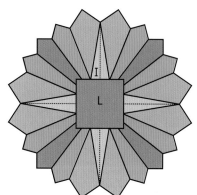

Block 16

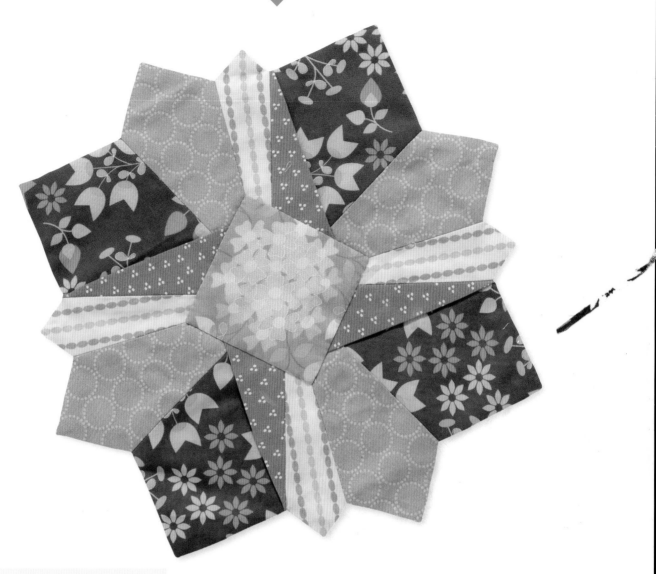

TEMPLATES NEEDED

Wedges:

4 of A1

4 of A2

4 of A5

Inserts: 4 of I (asymmetrical)

See "Asymmetrical Inserts,"
page 20.

Center: 1 of L

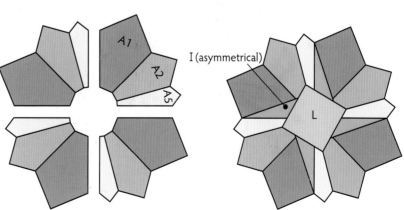

Block 17

TEMPLATES NEEDED

Wedges:

5 of B1

10 of B2

Inserts: 5 of I

Center: 1 of M

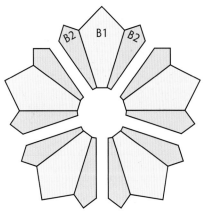

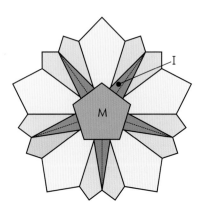

Block 18

TEMPLATES NEEDED

Wedges:

5 of B1

5 of B2

10 of B3

Inserts: None

Center: 1 of M

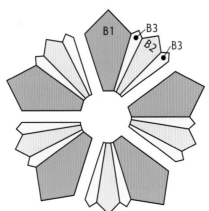

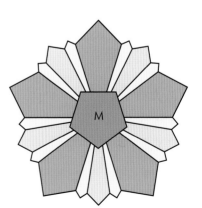

Block 19

TEMPLATES NEEDED

Wedges:

15 of F1

10 of F2

Inserts: 5 of I

Center: 1 each of M and N

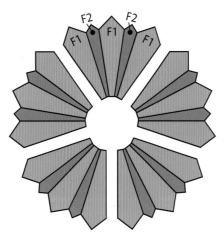

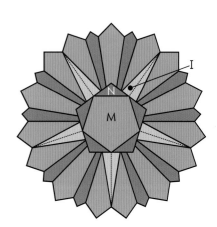

Block 20

TEMPLATES NEEDED

Wedges:

5 of F1

5 of F1 (flat)

20 of F2

Inserts: None

Center: 1 of M

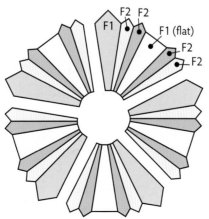

Block 21

TEMPLATES NEEDED

Wedges:

5 of A1

15 of A8

Inserts: None

Center: 1 of M

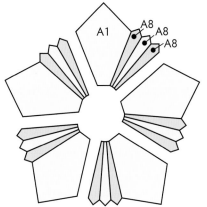

Block 22

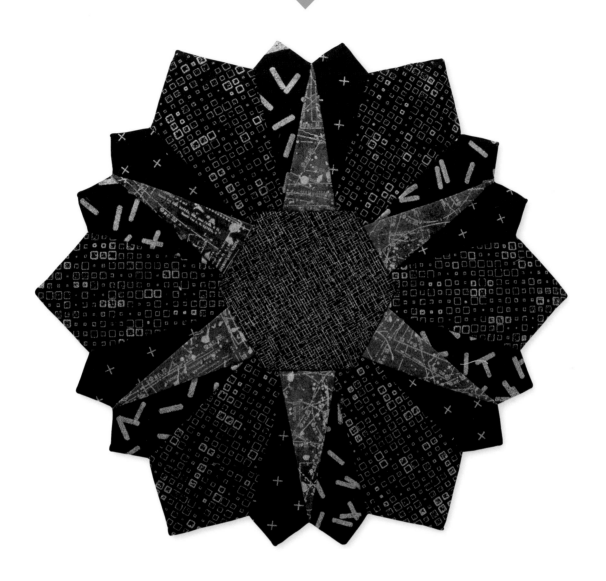

TEMPLATES NEEDED

Wedges:

6 of C1

12 of C4

Inserts: 6 of I

Center: 1 of O

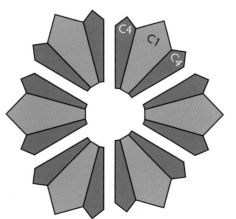

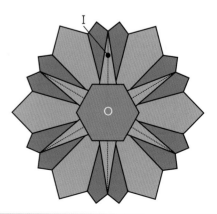

Block 23

TEMPLATES NEEDED

Wedges:

6 of A2

18 of A7

Inserts: None

Center: 1 of O

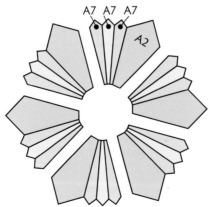

Block 24

TEMPLATES NEEDED

Wedges:

6 of E1

12 of E2

6 of E3 (flat)

Inserts: None

Center: 1 of O

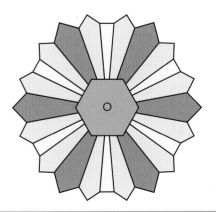

E3 (flat)

E2

E1

E2

Block 25

TEMPLATES NEEDED

Wedges:

6 of C1

6 of C3

6 of C6

Inserts: 6 of I (asymmetrical) See "Asymmetrical Inserts," page 20.

Center: 1 of O

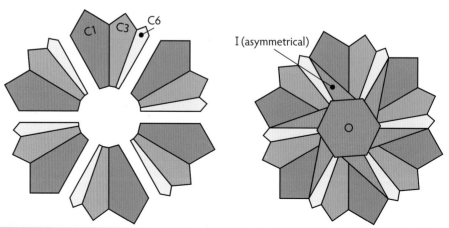

Block 26

TEMPLATES NEEDED

Wedges:

12 of G1

6 of G2

12 of G2 (flat)

Inserts: 6 of I

Center: 1 of O

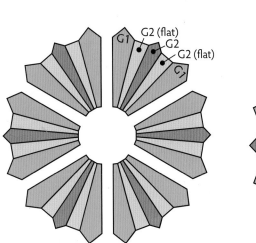

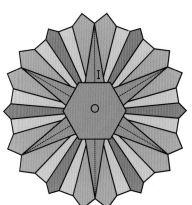

The Projects

Good Morning Place Mats

Reminiscent of a bright and sunny morning in the garden, these place mats are sure to give everyone at your table a cheerful start to the day.

Finished place mats: Set of 4 place mats, each 18" × 13½"

Blocks: Four 2-faceted Distinctive Dresden blocks

Blocks used: 2, 3, 4, and 5

Materials

Yardage is based on 42"-wide fabric.

1 yard *total* of assorted yellow and orange print scraps for blocks

Additional: 1 fat eighth (9" × 21") of yellow or orange print for *each* selected block with inserts

48 squares, 5" × 5", of assorted cream and white prints for backgrounds*

1⅜ yards of cream print for backing

32" × 42" piece of batting

Precut squares are perfect for this project.

Cutting

From the cream backing fabric, cut:
4 pieces, 16" × 21"

From the batting, cut:
4 pieces, 16" × 21"

Piecing the Blocks

Refer to "Techniques for Distinctive Dresdens" on page 11 for detailed instructions as needed.

While I used 2-faceted blocks 2–5, you can choose any four blocks you like from the block patterns on pages 25–51. Make the required templates for each block, and cut the pieces from the assorted yellow and orange prints. Assemble each block.

Assembling the Place Mats

Use a ¼" seam allowance throughout.

1. Choose 12 of the assorted cream and white 5" squares, and lay them out in three rows of four squares each. Join the squares into rows, alternating the pressing direction from row to row. Join the rows to complete the background unit, and press the seam allowances in one direction. Make four pieces that measure 14" × 18½", including seam allowances, for the place-mat backgrounds.

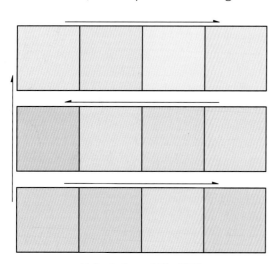

Make 4 pieces, 14" × 18½".

2. Referring to "Appliqué" on page 81, appliqué each block to a background unit to make four place-mat tops. If you choose to have some of the Dresden blocks run off the edge of the place mats, as I did, trim the overlapping block edges even with the background.

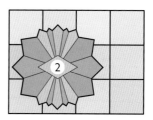

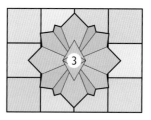

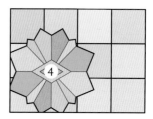

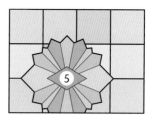

Appliqué 1 of each unit.

Finishing the Place Mats

1. Place a 16" × 21" piece of batting on a flat surface. Lay a 16" × 21" piece of backing fabric right side up on top of the batting. Center a place-mat top, right side *down,* on top of the backing. Pin around the edges.

2. Sew around the edges of the place-mat top using a ¼" seam allowance. Leave a 5" to 6" opening along one edge for turning.

3. Referring to the diagram, trim the backing and batting even with the place-mat top. On the back side, trim the batting again, close to the sewing line, being careful not to cut into the fabric layers. Clip the four corners at an angle to reduce bulk.

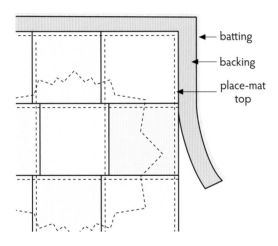

batting
backing
place-mat top

4. Turn the place mat right side out through the opening and press. Hand stitch the opening closed.

5. Quilt as desired. Using an erasable fabric marker, I drew lines radiating from the points of the blocks to suggest rays of sunshine. I then quilted within each of the spaces created by my lines, outlining each space and staying about ¼" away from the blocks, the edges of the place mat, and the space for the next radiating line.

6. Repeat steps 1–5 to finish each place mat.

Paper Lanterns Wall Quilt

I have a distinct memory from my childhood in Germany of celebrating Saint Martin's Day on November 11. Saint Martin rode in on his horse, giving candy to the boys and girls, but the image that endures in my mind most vividly is of the paper lanterns carried by the children. The lanterns were beautifully colored and were lit with candles, filling the night with glowing light. The more I thought about my Distinctive Dresden blocks, the more I was reminded of those paper lanterns of my childhood.

Finished quilt: 63" × 31"

Blocks: Seven assorted 3-, 4-, 5-, and 6-faceted Distinctive Dresden blocks

Blocks used: 7, 14, 15, 16, 19, 25, and 26

Materials

Yardage is based on 42"-wide fabric.

1¾ yards *total* of assorted gray, black, and coral print scraps for blocks

Additional: 1 fat eighth (9" × 21") of gray, black, or coral print for *each* selected block with inserts

1 fat quarter (18" × 21") of gray print for lantern-hanger bias strips

2¼ yards of off-white print for background and binding

2⅛ yards of fabric for backing

37" × 69" piece of batting

⅜" bias tape maker

Cutting

From the off-white print, cut:

1 piece, 31" × 63" (cut lengthwise)

5 strips, 2⅛" × 42" (cut widthwise)

Piecing the Blocks

Refer to "Techniques for Distinctive Dresdens" on page 11 for detailed instructions as needed.

Choose seven assorted blocks (in any combination) from the block patterns on pages 25–51. Make the required templates for each block, and cut the pieces from the assorted gray, black, and coral prints. Assemble each block.

Assembling the Quilt Top

Use a ¼" seam allowance throughout.

1. Lay the off-white 31" × 63" piece on a table, and place pins along the top edge of the fabric to indicate the placement of the lantern-hanger bias strips at 9", 17½", 23½", 34", 46", and 54" from the left edge.

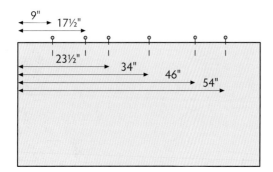

2. Referring to the manufacturer's directions for the ⅜" bias tape maker, use the gray fat quarter to make one bias strip in each of the following lengths: 4", 5", 7½", 12½", 15", and 18".

3. Referring to "Appliqué" on page 81 and the diagram below, appliqué the bias strips in their proper positions on the background.

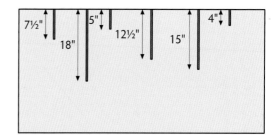

4. Pin the blocks to the background as shown, covering the raw ends of the bias strips. Notice that one block doesn't have a bias strip, but rather extends off the top of the background fabric. Trim the overlapping block (without a corresponding bias strip) even with the background's top edge. Appliqué the blocks in place, again referring to "Appliqué."

Finishing the Quilt

1. Layer the quilt top, batting, and backing. Quilt as desired. I quilted random crisscross lines across the quilt background, radiating outward from the seams between some of the block wedges.

2. Referring to "Traditional Double-Fold Binding" on page 83, use the off-white 2⅛"-wide strips to bind the quilt.

QUICK MINI QUILT

Choose any single Dresden block to make a stunning mini wall hanging or table topper. Make a bias-strip hanger the desired length and stitch it to the quilt back. Appliqué your assembled block off-center on the background, and then follow these project directions for a quick finish.

Quilt size: 18½" × 21½"

Merry Christmas Tree Skirt

This pretty tree skirt, along with twinkling stars, icy snowflakes, and frosted cookies of the season, makes visions of Christmas complete.

Finished tree skirt: 51½" in diameter

Blocks: Two *each* of three 3-faceted Distinctive Dresden blocks

Blocks used: 6, 8, and 10

Materials

Yardage is based on 42"-wide fabric unless otherwise specified.

1½ yards *total* of assorted aqua, red, and cream print scraps for blocks

Additional: 1 fat eighth (9" × 21") of aqua, red, or cream print for *each* selected block with inserts

1⅔ yards of 54"- to 60"-wide red cotton/linen blend fabric for background

⅔ yard of red check for bias binding

1¾ yards of 54"- to 60"-wide fabric for backing

51" × 58" piece of batting

6 yards of aqua ¼"-wide rickrack

¾"-diameter cream button

Acrylic rulers: 60° triangle and 6" × 24" rectangle

Pencils and string, or compass ruler

Cutting

From the red check, cut *on the bias:*

2⅛"-wide strips to total 220" in length

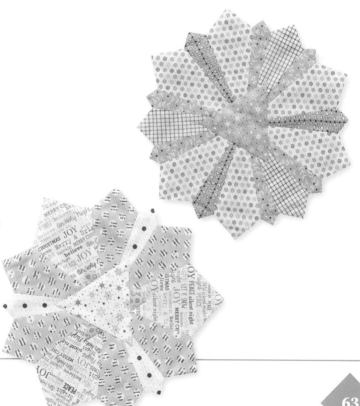

Piecing the Blocks

Refer to "Techniques for Distinctive Dresdens" on page 11 for detailed instructions as needed.

Choose three 3-faceted blocks from the block patterns on pages 25–51, as they will work best in the large triangles. Make the required templates for two of each block, and cut the pieces from the assorted aqua, red, and cream prints. Assemble two of each block.

Assembling the Tree Skirt

Use a ¼" seam allowance throughout.

1. Fold the red cotton/linen piece in half, aligning the selvages. Using a 60° triangle ruler and a 6" × 24" ruler to extend your lines, mark and cut three equilateral triangles that measure 26" along each edge. (Since the fabric is folded, this will result in six triangles total.)

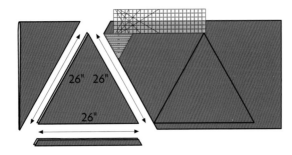

2. Measure 15" down from the top point of each red triangle, and mark with a pin to indicate the block's center point.

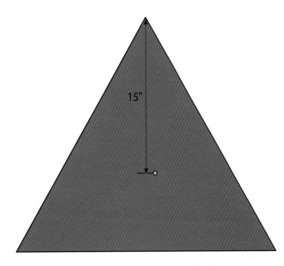

3. Referring to "Appliqué" on page 81 and using the marked center points for placement guidance, appliqué a block to each red triangle.

4. Sew the appliquéd triangles together, leaving one seam completely open, and the last 2" open at the center for each of the other seams. Press the seam allowances open.

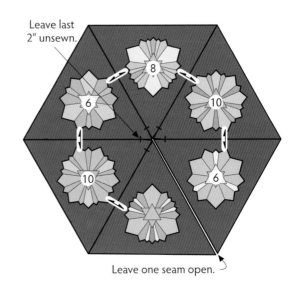

Leave last 2" unsewn.

Leave one seam open.

Trimming the Curves

1. With right sides together, fold the tree-skirt top in half and then in thirds along the seamlines to make a triangle. Place the triangle on your work surface with the 2" seam openings at the top. Mark 15" down from the top of the triangle. Use pencils and string or a compass ruler to draw a circle that radiates from the 15" mark and meets the outside edges of the folded triangle; the circle should have a radius of approximately 7½" (15" diameter).

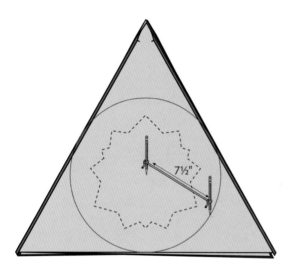

2. Measuring from each bottom corner of the folded triangle, use the pencils and string or compass ruler to draw a curved line between the drawn circle and the outer edge of the triangle.

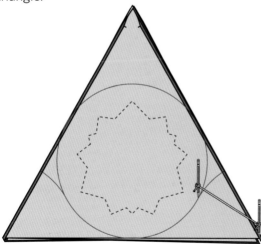

3. Place a small plate (approximately 5" in diameter) at the top corner of the folded triangle, positioning the lower edge of the plate just below the 2" seam openings. Trace along the edge of the plate.

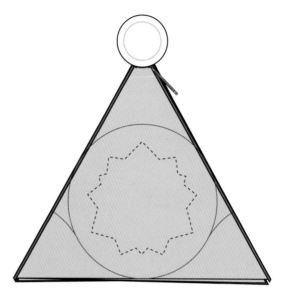

4. Cut through all layers on the marked lines as indicated in the diagram to create the scalloped outer edge and the center opening.

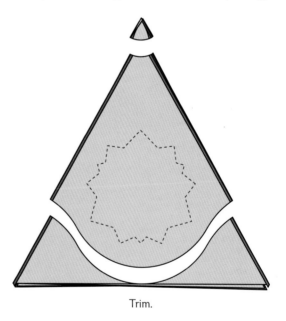

Trim.

Finishing the Tree Skirt

1. Layer the tree skirt top, batting, and backing. Quilt as desired. In the red background, I quilted straight lines radiating from the center opening, randomly quilting circular shapes along the lines for interest.

2. Trim the batting and backing even with all edges of the tree-skirt top, including the open seam and the center opening.

3. Referring to "Bias Binding for Curves" on page 85, use the checked 2⅛"-wide bias strips to bind the tree skirt, including the open seam and the center opening. Instead of sewing the binding to the front of the tree skirt as usual, sew it to the back.

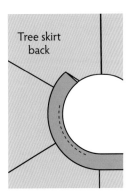

4. Sew the folded edge of the binding to the front of the tree skirt by machine, inserting the aqua rickrack under the edge of the binding as you go. Stop stitching at the right corner of the center opening.

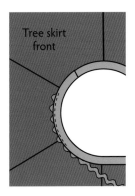

5. Create a ¾"-long loop of rickrack, backstitching to secure the loop. Continue stitching the remaining binding and rickrack in place.

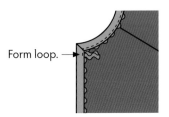

Form loop. →

6. Sew the cream button to the corner opposite the rickrack loop.

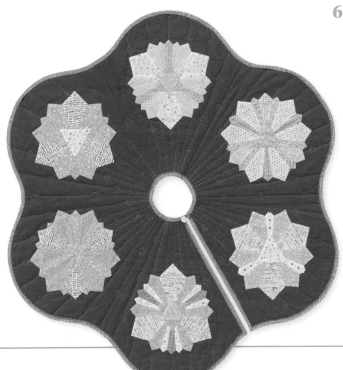

Clamoring for More Quilt

Like pearls in their oysters, these Distinctive Dresden blocks are nestled on a bed of luscious wool, showing off their splendor. Once you start, you too will be "clam"-oring for more.

Finished quilt: 45½" × 53"

Blocks: Assorted 5- and 6-faceted Distinctive Dresden blocks: ten full blocks, five half blocks, and two quarter blocks

Blocks used: 18, 20, 21, 23, and 24. For the number of each, see step 1 on page 69.

Materials

Yardage is based on 42"-wide fabric unless otherwise specified.

3¼ yards *total* of assorted print scraps for blocks

Additional: 1 fat eighth (9" × 21") of print fabric for *each* selected block with inserts

½ yard *each* of 9 assorted bright 100% wool fabrics, 54"-wide, for block backgrounds, pieced background, and binding

3¼ yards of fabric for backing

52" × 59" piece of batting

Assorted colors of 8-weight variegated pearl cotton thread

Pencils and string, or compass ruler

Cutting

From the assorted bright wools, cut:

9 squares, 16" × 16"

5 rectangles, 8½" × 16"

2 squares, 8½" × 8½"

21 squares, 8" × 8"

1⅜"-wide strips to total 210" in length

Piecing the Blocks

Refer to "Techniques for Distinctive Dresdens" on page 11 for detailed instructions as needed.

1. Choose five 5- and 6-faceted blocks from the block patterns on pages 25–51. Make the required templates for 10 full blocks, five half blocks, and two quarter blocks. (For the full blocks, I made one of block 20; two *each* of blocks 18, 21, and 23; and three of block 24. For the half blocks, I made one *each* of blocks 21, 23, and 24 and two of block 20. For the quarter blocks, I made two of block 23.) When using 5-faceted block designs, you'll need to make 3 facets for a half block or 2 facets for a quarter block; for 6-faceted block designs, construct 3 facets for a half block or 2 facets for a quarter block. You will trim the excess as needed during quilt assembly. Cut the pieces from the assorted prints. When preparing pieces for the half and quarter blocks, add ¼" seam allowance (instead of ⅜") to the edges that will be along the outside of the quilt top.

2. Assemble 10 full, five half, and two quarter blocks.

Assembling the Quilt Top

1. Use pencils and string or a compass ruler to draw a circle template with a 7½" radius (15" diameter) onto a large piece of paper. Cut out the template, and use it to cut nine full-block backgrounds from the 16" wool squares.

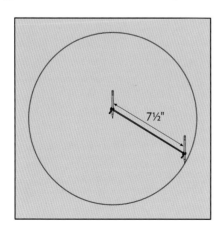

2. Fold the circle template in half, and use it to cut five half-block backgrounds from the 8½" × 16" wool rectangles, adding a ¼" seam allowance along the straight edge.

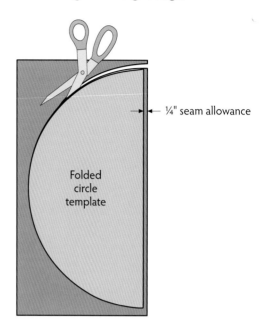

¼" seam allowance

Folded circle template

3. Fold the circle template in half again to make a quarter circle, and use it to cut two quarter-block backgrounds from the 8½" wool squares, adding a ¼" seam allowance along each straight edge.

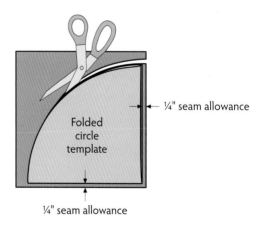

¼" seam allowance

Folded circle template

¼" seam allowance

4. Fold each full-block background into quarters along the grain lines to create light creases; unfold and mark the quarter points with pins. Fold each half-block background in half along the grain lines, unfold, and mark the center with a pin. These marks will be used to align the "clams" and also to orient the block onto the background.

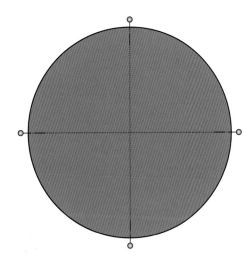

5. Lay out the 21 wool 8" squares in six rows of graduating lengths as shown. Using a ¼" seam allowance, sew the squares together into rows, and then join the rows to make a pieced background. Press all seam allowances open to reduce bulk.

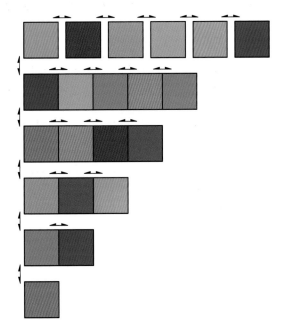

6. Referring to "Appliqué" on page 81, appliqué nine full blocks and five half blocks onto the wool backgrounds from step 4, and appliqué the two quarter blocks onto the wool backgrounds from step 3 (set aside the remaining full block for step 10). When aligning the half and quarter blocks, remember that the center of the block is ¼" in from the straight edges of the wool backgrounds. Trim the excess from the half and quarter blocks as needed.

7. Lay out the appliquéd full, half, and quarter circles, using the diagram as a guide. Start in the upper-right corner to accommodate the overlaps. Thread baste the pieces together along the edges to make the clams section. The unit should measure 45½" × 52¾".

8. Appliqué the remaining full block in place near the upper-left corner of the pieced background. Thread baste the clams section onto the edge of the pieced background.

9. Using a herringbone stitch and assorted colors of 8-weight pearl cotton, stitch the raw edges of the wool block backgrounds to the layer underneath. I varied the size of my stitches for interest.

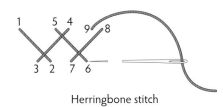

Herringbone stitch

10. Remove the basting stitches. Trim away the excess overlapped areas of the block backgrounds on the back of the quilt.

LET THE STITCHING SHOW!

If, like me, you want your herringbone stitches to really show, use pearl cotton colors that contrast with the wool background colors. In many cases I used variegated pearl cotton for an extra bit of playfulness.

Finishing the Quilt

1. Piece the quilt backing using one horizontal seam. Press.

2. Layer the quilt top, batting, and backing. Quilt as desired. I quilted two parallel lines through the center of each vertical row in the pieced background. I added two lines of quilting near the edge of each wool block background.

3. Referring to "Single-Fold Binding" on page 85, use the assorted wool 1⅜"-wide strips to bind the quilt.

Over the Edge Table Runner

When I lecture, I often mention that I love quilted items with unusual finishes instead of the traditional borders and binding. Being true to form, you might say I've gone "over the edge" on this unique table runner.

Finished table runner: 12" × 36"
(including the overhanging wedges)

Blocks: Three 4-faceted Distinctive Dresden blocks

Blocks used: 11, 12, and 13

Materials

Yardage is based on 42"-wide fabric.

¾ yard *total* of assorted teal print scraps for blocks

Additional: 1 fat eighth (9" × 21") of teal print for *each* selected block with inserts

¾ yard of gray shot cotton for background and backing

15" × 39" piece of batting

Erasable fabric marker

6" × 24" acrylic ruler

Cutting

From the gray shot cotton, cut:

2 rectangles, 11½" × 35½"

Piecing the Blocks

Refer to "Techniques for Distinctive Dresdens" on page 11 for detailed instructions as needed.

I chose three 4-faceted blocks for this project so that only the widest wedges in the block would extend over the quilt sides. Choose your blocks from the patterns on pages 25–51. Make the required templates for each block, and cut the pieces from the assorted teal prints. (The blocks in this project hang over the edge of the background, so each extending wedge needs to have a finished, or covered, backing. Refer to "Making Covered-Back Wedges" on page 21 to prepare the extending wedges for each block.) Assemble each block.

Assembling the Table Runner

1. Place the batting on a flat surface. Lay one gray 11½" × 35½" rectangle right side up on top of the batting. Place the remaining gray 11½" × 35½" rectangle right side *down* on top of the first rectangle, aligning all the raw edges. Pin around the edges.

2. Sew around the edges of the gray rectangles using a ¼" seam allowance. Leave a 5" to 6" opening along one edge for turning.

3. Trim the batting very close to the sewing line, being careful not to cut into the fabric layers. Clip the four corners at an angle to reduce bulk.

4. Turn the table runner right side out through the opening and press. Hand stitch the opening closed.

Finishing the Table Runner

1. Using an erasable fabric marker and a 6" × 24" ruler, draw a line along the lengthwise center of the table runner.

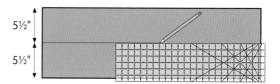

2. In the same manner, draw a line along the center width of the table runner.

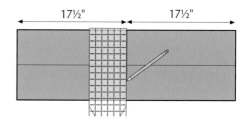

3. Pin the center block to the background, aligning the longest wedges of the block with the marked lines and allowing the covered-back wedges to flow off the edges of the background as shown. Align and pin the remaining blocks on each side of the center block, with the inner wedges touching and the covered-back wedges flowing off the edges of the background.

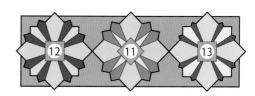

4. Referring to "Appliqué" on page 81, appliqué the blocks to the background. Make sure to appliqué only through the background layer to ensure that your stitches do not show on the backing. On the back of the runner, whipstitch the edge of the backing rectangle to the underside of each wedge that extends off the runner to secure them in place.

5. Quilt as desired. I quilted in the ditch around each block and block center, to make the blocks "pop" forward and help them stand out from the background.

Class-Act Cushions

Stunning, stylish, and distinctive, these cushions will add a touch of chic to any decor! Understated elegance abounds with the use of lustrous metallic fabrics combined with neutral cotton/linen blends.

Finished cushions:
pentagon, 18½" × 19½" × 2"
hexagon, 17" × 19½" × 2"
square, 17½" × 17½" × 2"
triangle, 18¾" × 21" × 2"

Blocks: 1 *each* of 2-, 3-, 5-, and 6-faceted blocks

Blocks used: 1, 9, 17, and 22

Materials

Yardage is based on 42"-wide fabric.

For one cushion:

¼ yard *total* of assorted metallic print scraps for block

Additional: 1 fat eighth (9" × 21") of metallic print for *each* selected block with inserts

1⅝ yards of cotton/linen blend fabric for background, backing, and gusset

1½ yards of muslin for cushion insert (optional)

2½ yards of 22"-wide high-loft polyester batting

Zipper to coordinate with cotton/linen blend (14" for triangle and square, 12" for pentagon, 9" for hexagon)

1 bag of polyester fiberfill

6" × 24" acrylic ruler

Cutting

From the cotton/linen blend, cut:
2 squares, 22" × 22"
2 strips, 2½" × 42"
1 strip, 2" × 42"

2. Layer the cushion top and the remaining cotton/linen 22" square with wrong sides together. To trim each edge and create your desired cushion shape, align the tips of two of the block's widest wedges with the lines on a 6" × 24" ruler, and cut at the measurement indicated in the diagram for your selected cushion shape. Continue rotating the ruler to cut adjacent edges using the tips of the widest wedges as your guide. (For the triangle cushion, round off the points of the triangle by tracing around a large dinner plate.)

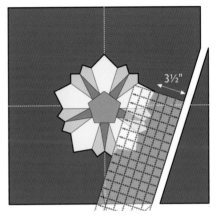

Trim.

Piecing the Block

Refer to "Techniques for Distinctive Dresdens" on page 11 for detailed instructions as needed.

Referring to the block patterns on pages 25–51, choose one block for your desired cushion: a 2-faceted block for the square, a 3-faceted block for the triangle, a 5-faceted block for the pentagon, or a 6-faceted block for the hexagon. Make the required templates for the block, and cut the pieces from the assorted metallic prints. Assemble the block.

Assembling the Cushion Cover

1. Fold one cotton/linen 22" square into quarters to find the center; unfold. Pin the block to the square, using the fold lines to center it. Referring to "Appliqué" on page 81, appliqué the block in place to make the cushion top.

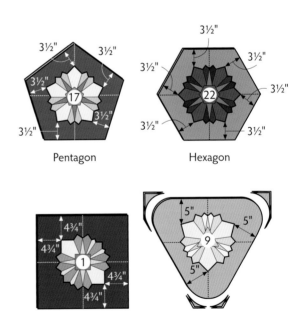

Pentagon   Hexagon

Square   Triangle

Make 1 of your selected
cushion shape.

3. Cut four layers of high-loft batting using the trimmed cushion top as a template. Set aside.

4. From the 2" × 42" strip of cotton/linen fabric, cut two pieces the same length as your zipper. Turn under ¼" along one long edge of each strip and press. Using a zipper foot, sew a fabric strip to each side of the zipper, with the folded-under edge along the zipper teeth. Press, using a press cloth to protect the zipper teeth. Trim the zipper unit to 2½" wide, centering the 1¼" mark of a ruler on the center of the zipper teeth.

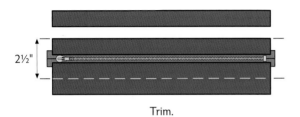

2½"

Trim.

5. Using a ¼" seam allowance, sew a cotton/linen 2½" × 42" strip to each end of the zipper unit to make the gusset.

6. Pin the gusset around the cushion top, centering the zipper unit along one side so that the zipper itself does not continue around the corner. Stitch the layers together, stopping ¼" from the corner. Leave the needle in the fabric, raise the presser foot, and then pivot the cushion top, aligning the raw edges of the gusset with the raw edges of the next side of the cushion top. Continue to the next corner. Stop sewing where the ends of the gusset strips meet.

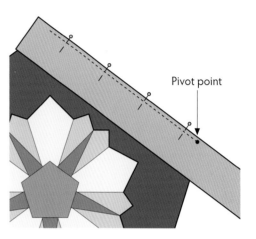

Pivot point

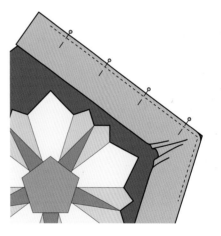

7. Stitch across the ends of the gusset strip and trim the excess fabric, leaving ¼" seam allowances.

8. Unzip the zipper so that the cushion can be turned right side out. With right sides together, layer the cushion top/gusset unit from step 7 on the cushion back from step 2, aligning the corners. Pin the layers together and stitch all the way around, pivoting at the corners to make the cushion cover.

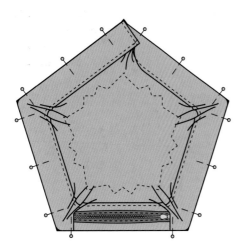

9. If desired, finish the seam allowances with a serger or zigzag stitch. Turn the cushion cover right side out. Press the seams with a sleeve board, or by placing a towel under the seams.

Finishing the Cushion

1. Place the four layers of high-loft batting inside the cushion cover; this is easiest if you fold the stack of batting into thirds, and then unfold the stack once it's inside the cushion, easing the batting layers against the edges of the gusset.

2. Gently separate the batting layers to find the middle, and insert fiberfill as needed to fill out the cushion.

3. Close the zipper.

OPTIONAL CUSHION INSERT

You may wish to make a muslin cushion insert to keep things tidy and allow for easy washing of the cushion cover. Assemble the insert in the same manner as the cushion cover, but don't add a zipper unit to the gusset. Follow finishing steps 1 and 2 above to stuff the insert with batting and fiberfill. Sew the opening closed by hand or machine, and slip it inside the cushion cover.

Quiltmaking Basics

Here I discuss a few quiltmaking techniques as they pertain to the projects in this book. For more details, go to ShopMartingale.com/HowtoQuilt for free, downloadable information about many other quilting topics.

Appliqué

For all the projects in this book, the edges that will be appliquéd are already turned under. If you haven't done so yet, press the edges to be appliquéd with Best Press (page 9), and carefully remove the paper templates by sliding a tailor's awl under the fabric edge to loosen the paper.

1. Pin the appliqué in place using appliqué pins. Thread your needle using a single strand of thread that closely matches the color of the appliqué fabric, and tie a knot in one end. Hide the knot in the fold made by the seam allowance, bringing the needle out along the folded edge.

   When I'm appliquéing blocks with contrasting colors and values, I change thread color as needed. Instead of tying off my thread between wedges, I use a locking backstitch (see step 6 on page 17) on the back side of my work to secure the thread.

Then I make running stitches through the background fabric to the next wedge requiring the same color. Before I resume appliquéing, I add another locking backstitch to ensure the thread will not loosen.

2. Make the first stitch into the background fabric, directly below where the needle emerged. Run the needle not more than ⅛" under your background fabric, parallel to the edge of the appliqué. Bring the needle up through the background fabric, catching only one or two threads of the folded edge of the appliqué. Very gently tug the thread with each stitch.

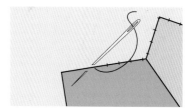

Appliqué stitch

3. When the appliqué is complete, bring your needle to the back and create two locking backstitches, as described in "Joining Wedges with English Paper Piecing," step 6, on page 17.

Backing

The quilt backing needs to be at least 6" larger than the quilt top (3" on all sides). With small items such as table runners and place mats, a backing 4" larger than the item is sufficient. However, if you plan to have your quilt professionally machine quilted, check with the quilter to see how you should prepare your backing.

If your quilt is wider than 40", you'll need to piece the backing. The seam can be placed vertically or horizontally. For larger quilts, it is usually necessary to sew two or three lengths together to make a backing that is large enough.

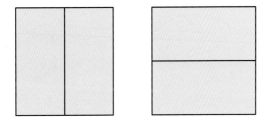

Trim away the selvages before piecing the lengths together. I press the seam allowances open to reduce bulk and make quilting easier. Extra blocks or leftovers from piecing the quilt top can be pieced into the backing fabric to create wonderful art on the quilt back.

Batting

I use different types of batting depending upon the project I am making. For a baby quilt, I may use 100% polyester for easy washing. In small projects, such as a table runner, place mat, or anything else that doesn't require a lot of weight or thickness, I use Hobbs Thermore batting. For a large bed quilt, I prefer to use 100% cotton batting or an 80/20 cotton/polyester blend. Whichever batting you choose, make sure to follow the manufacturer's directions for how closely it should be quilted and how it should be laundered.

PREWASH BATTING?

Although I don't prewash my batting, some people like to. If you do, make sure to follow the manufacturer's directions, but never agitate batting when wet, before it is enclosed inside the quilt.

Basting and Layering

Quilting has come a long way since the days when basting could only be done with safety pins or thread. I prefer to use basting spray, since it's much quicker and easier than bending over tables or kneeling on the floor for hours. Be sure to follow the manufacturer's instructions for the product you are using. Here's how I spray baste a quilt.

1. Lay the backing fabric wrong side up on a flat, clean surface. Anchor it with masking tape or pins, being careful not to stretch the backing out of shape.

2. Spread the batting over the backing fabric, making sure the edges are parallel. Fold the batting back about halfway and spray the backing fabric evenly with basting spray. Unfold the batting back onto the backing fabric and gently smooth it in place, starting in the center and working outward. Repeat for the other half of the batting and backing.

3. Center the quilt top right side up on top of the batting. Fold the quilt top back about halfway. Spray the batting evenly with basting spray. Unfold the quilt top and gently smooth it in place, starting in the center and working outward. Repeat for the other half of the quilt top.

4. Remove the tape or pins. After the quilting is complete, trim the batting and backing even with the edges of the quilt top.

Traditional Double-Fold Binding

When I make a quilted item with traditional binding, as in the Paper Lanterns Wall Quilt (page 59), I use a double-fold binding and cut strips 2⅛" wide across the width of the fabric, which are then joined to make a continuous binding strip.

1. Layer two binding strips at right angles, right sides together, and stitch diagonally across the corner as shown. Trim the excess fabric, leaving ¼" for seam allowances. Press the seam allowances open to distribute bulk. Repeat, adding the remaining strips to make one long binding strip.

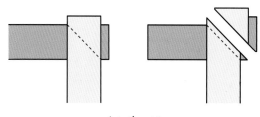

Join the strips.

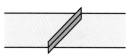

Press seam allowances open.

2. Press the binding strip in half lengthwise, wrong sides together and raw edges aligned.

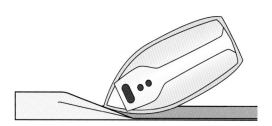

3. Starting near the center on one long side of the quilt top and leaving a 10" tail, stitch the binding to the quilt using a ¼" seam allowance. Stop stitching ¼" from the first corner and backstitch several stitches. Clip the thread and remove the quilt from the machine.

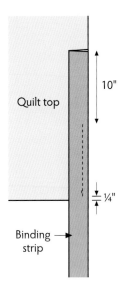

4. Fold the binding up away from the quilt, making a 45° angle with the fold.

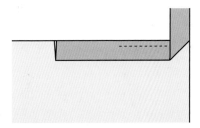

5. Fold the binding back down on itself, even with the raw edge of the quilt.

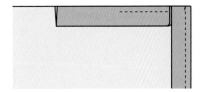

6. Beginning at the fold with a backstitch, stitch along the edge of the quilt top, stopping ¼" from the next corner as before. Repeat the process on the remaining sides of the quilt.

7. On the last side of the quilt, stop sewing at least 12" from where you started. Lay the quilt edge flat and overlap the starting and ending binding tails. Trim the ends so that the overlap is exactly the same distance as the cut width of your binding (2⅛" in this case).

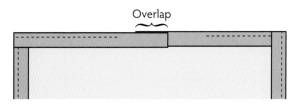

8. Open the two ends of the folded binding. Place the tails right sides together, overlapping them at right angles as shown. Sew a diagonal line from corner to corner. Trim the seam allowances to ¼". Press the seam allowances open.

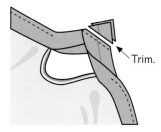

9. Refold the binding, align the raw edges with the raw edges of the quilt top, and finish sewing the binding in place.

10. Fold the binding over the raw edges of the quilt, with the folded edge covering the row of machine stitching. Hand stitch the binding to the quilt backing, folding the miters in place as you reach each corner.

Bias Binding for Curves

Binding items with curved edges means using bias strips that will stretch smoothly around the edges. The Merry Christmas Tree Skirt (page 63) was a perfect project for this technique. Bias binding is cut on the diagonal so that the threads of the fabric are at a 45° angle to the length of the strip. (Refer to the Rotary Cutting tutorial at ShopMartingale.com/HowtoQuilt for details about cutting bias strips.)

Bias binding is applied to the quilt exactly like traditional double-fold binding (page 83), with the following exceptions.

1. Ease a little extra fullness into outside curves to give it the extra room to fit smoothly along the edges.

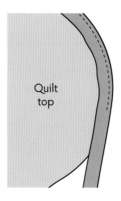

2. On inside curves, pull bias binding a little tighter to fit without pleats or folds.

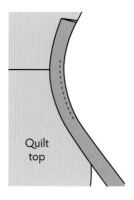

Single-Fold Binding

Single-fold binding is used for small items like miniature quilts, or where traditional double-fold binding may be problematic, such as in the Clamoring for More Quilt (page 67). In that project, the wool binding would have been far too bulky if it was doubled. Single-fold binding is cut much narrower, usually between 1" and 1½" wide, depending on the desired finished width.

1. Referring to step 1 of "Traditional Double-Fold Binding" on page 83, join the strips to make one long binding strip.

2. Do *not* press the binding strip in half lengthwise. Align one long edge of the binding strip with a long side of the quilt top. Referring to steps 3–9 of "Traditional Double-Fold Binding," sew the binding to the quilt top, turning the corners as directed.

3. Fold the binding over the raw edges of the quilt to cover the row of machine stitching. Turning the raw edge of the binding strip under ¼" as you go, hand stitch the binding to the quilt backing. Fold the miters in place as you reach each corner.

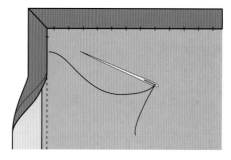

Hand stitch binding to quilt back.

Patterns

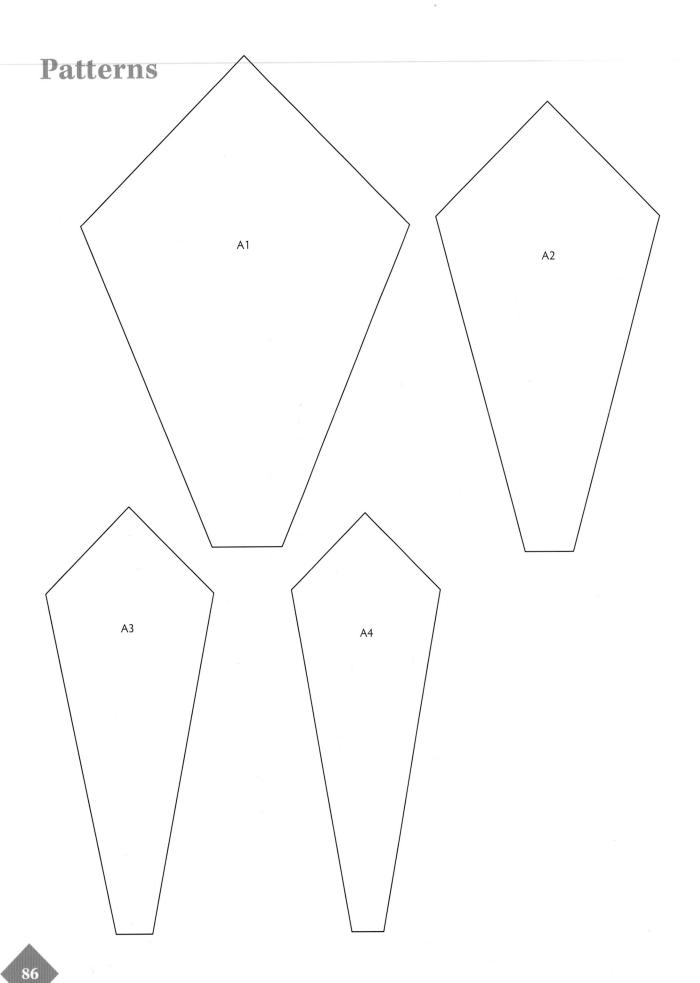

A1

A2

A3

A4

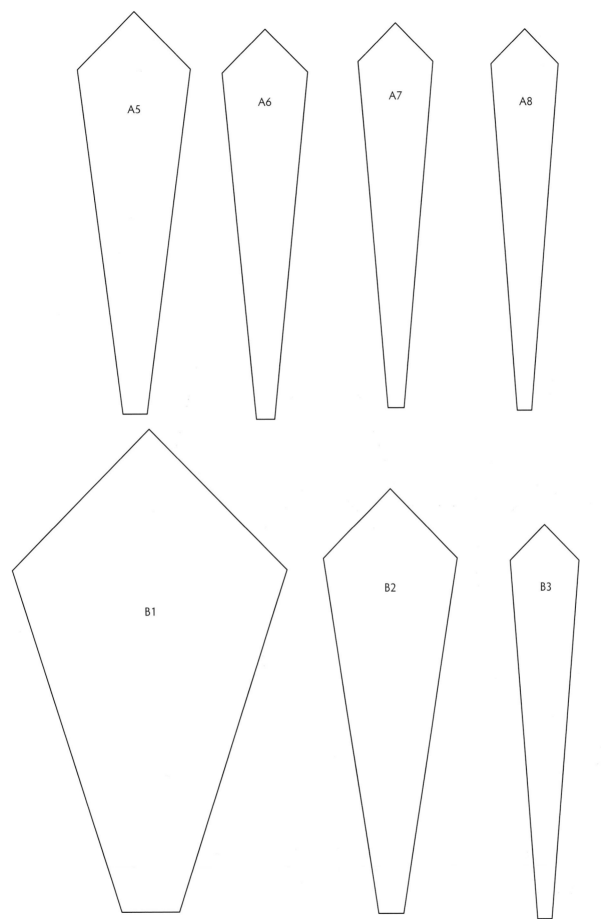

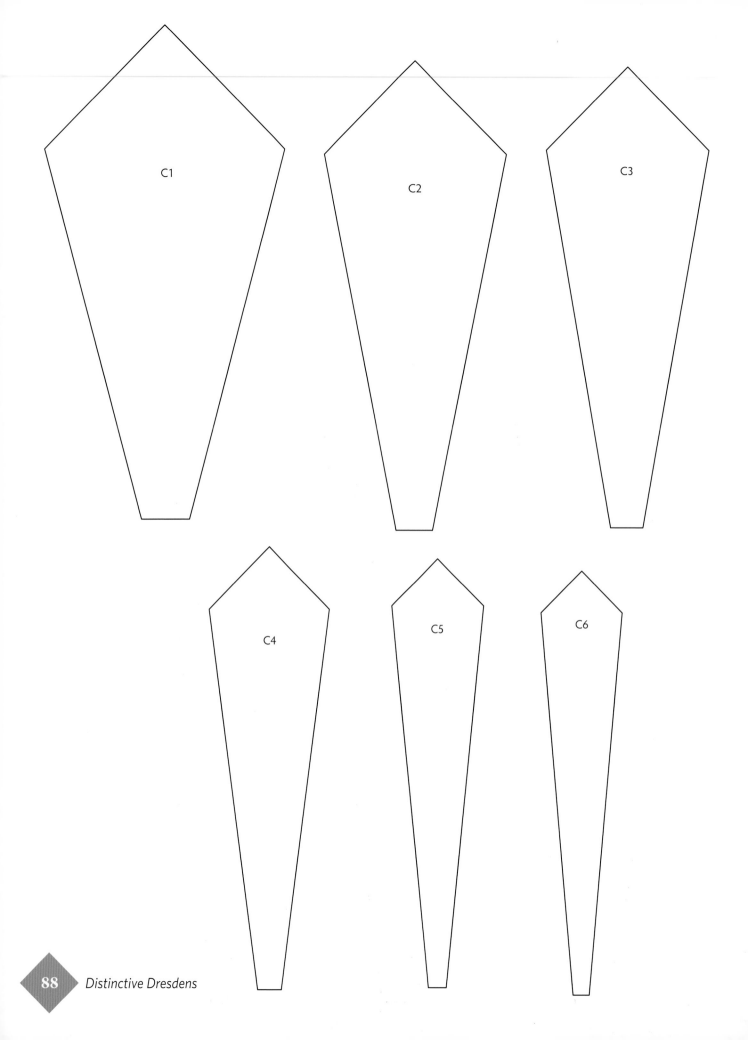

C1

C2

C3

C4

C5

C6

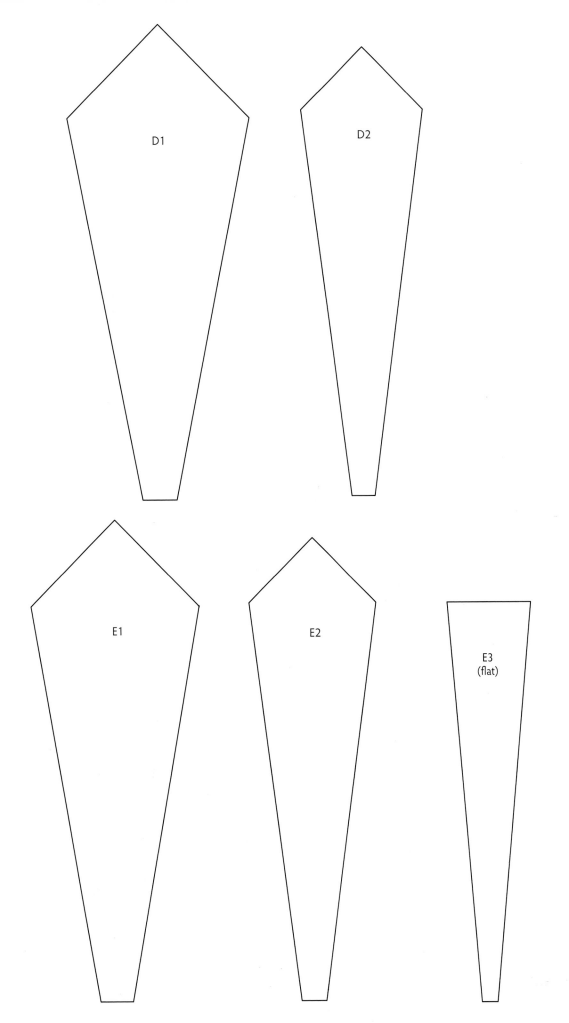

D1

D2

E1

E2

E3
(flat)

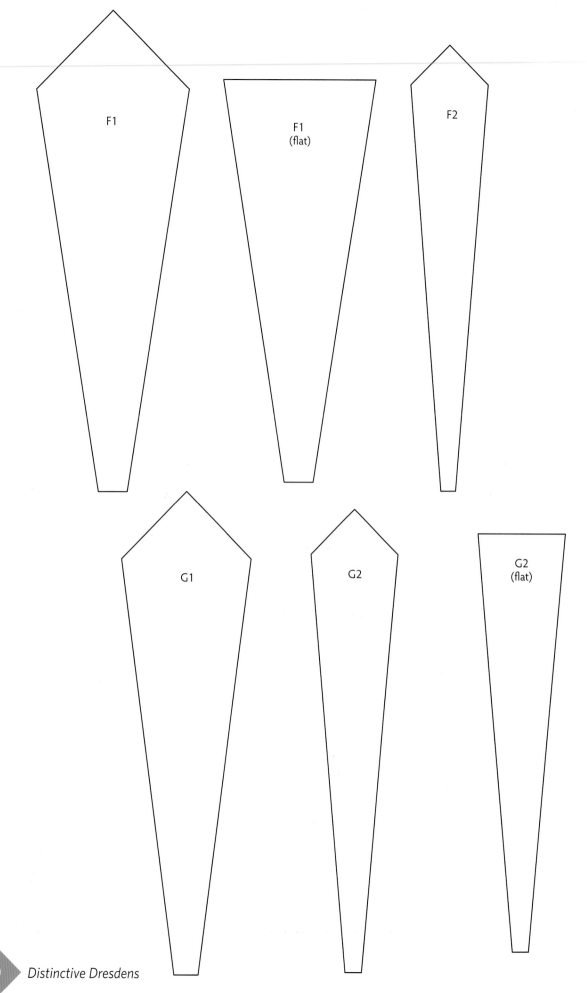

F1

F1
(flat)

F2

G1

G2

G2
(flat)

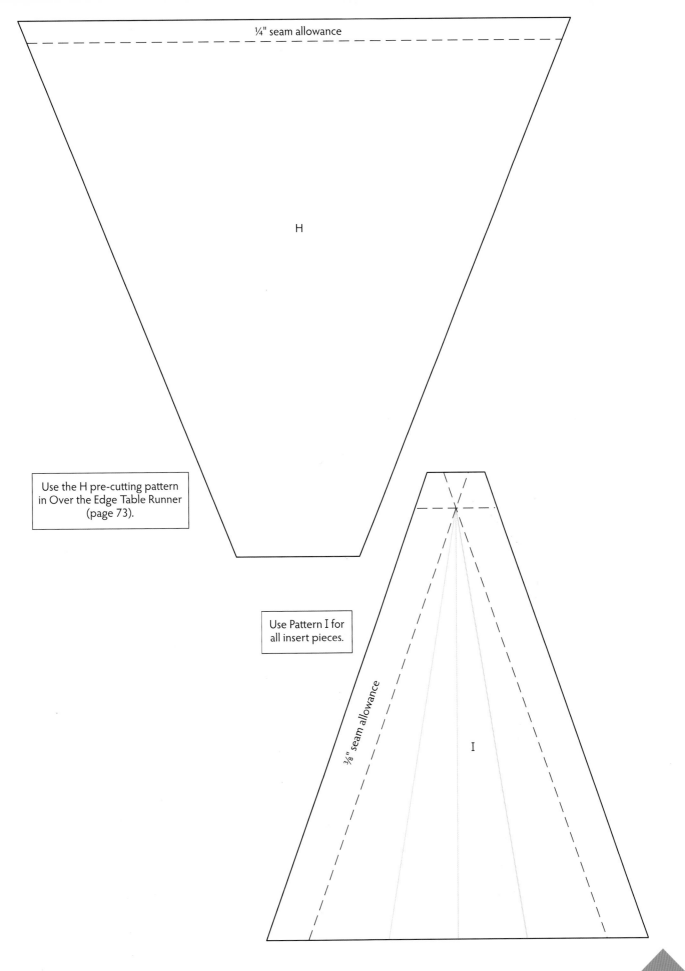

¼" seam allowance

H

Use the H pre-cutting pattern in Over the Edge Table Runner (page 73).

Use Pattern I for all insert pieces.

⅜" seam allowance

I

¼" seam allowance

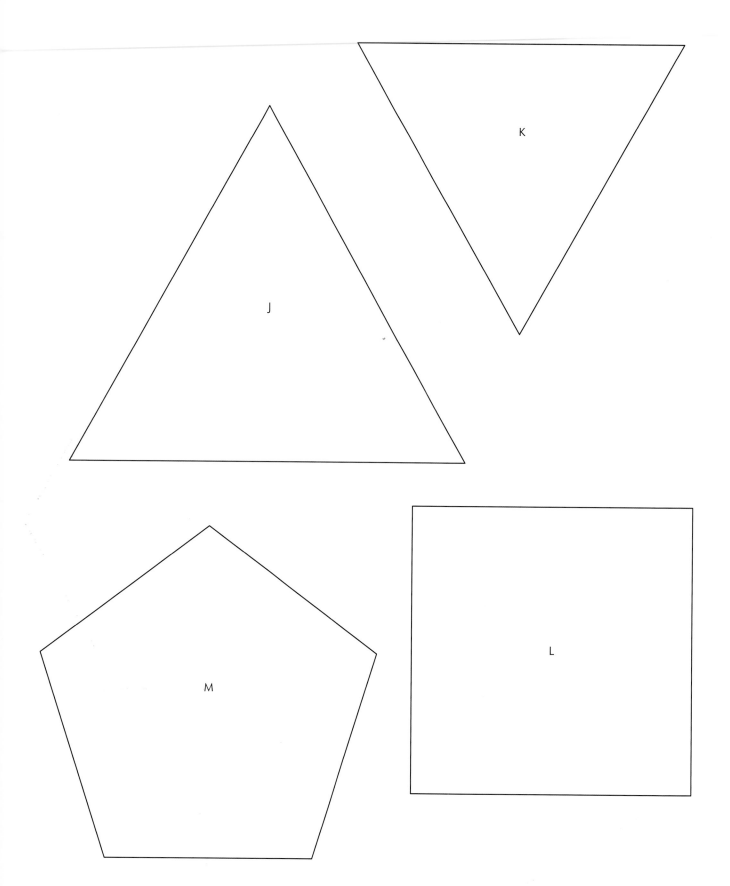

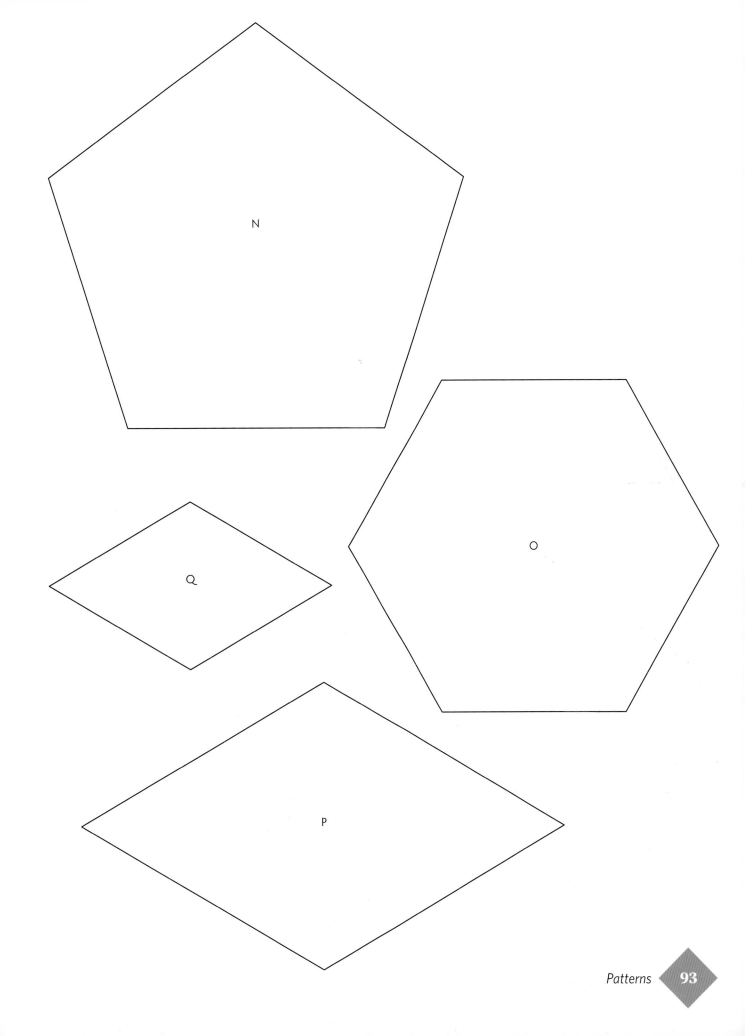

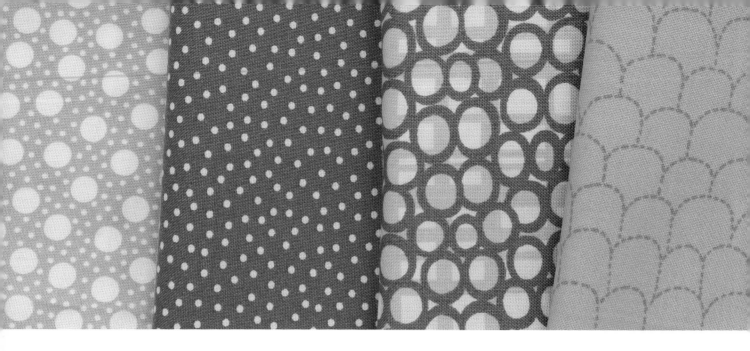

Resources

Many of the supplies referred to throughout the book are available at your local quilt shop. If you can't find them in your area, try these websites.

Aurifil
aurifil.com
50-weight 100% cotton thread

Clover
clover-usa.com
Appliqué pins, marking pens, needles, needle threader, Hera marker

CM Designs
addaquarter.com
Add-Three-Eighths ruler

Collins
prym-consumer-usa.com
Fine-line water-erasable marking pen

Fons & Porter
shopfonsandporter.com
Water-soluble glue marker and refills

Hobbs Batting
hobbsbondedfibers.com
Thermore 100% polyester batting

Katja's Quilt Shoppe
katjasquiltshoppe.com
General quilting supplies and fabric

Mary Ellen Products
maryellenproducts.com
Best Press spray starch

Mettler
amann-mettler.com
Silk-finish 50-weight 100% cotton thread

Odif USA
odifusa.com
Temporary fabric adhesive

Paper Pieces
paperpieces.com
Precut paper packs for English paper piecing

Sewline
sewline-product.com
Needle threader

Superior Threads
superiorthreads.com
50-weight 100% cotton thread

WonderFil
wonderfil.ca
InvisaFil 100-weight 2-ply polyester thread